I AM WONDERFUL

WONDERFUL: inspiring, delightful, pleasurable, extremely good, marvelous, admirable, excellent, astonishing, great, extraordinary

This book belongs to

____

____

I am fearfully and wonderfully made
(Psalm 139:14)

**I am the apple of God's eye
(Deuteronomy 32:10b) (Zachariah 2:8)**

I am beautiful and made without a flaw
(Song of Solomon 4:7)

I was created in the image of God
(Genesis 1:27)

I am strong and courageous, I am not afraid, for God is with me (Joshua 1:9)

I am valuable
(Luke 12:7)

I can do all things through Christ who strengthens me (Philippians 4:13)

NISH FINISH FINISH FIH FINISH FIN

He that is in me is greater
(1 John 4:4)

I am precious in God's eyes
(Isaiah 43:4)

God has a great plan for my life
(Jeremiah 29:11)

I am God's masterpiece and was created
to do good works (Ephesians 2:10)

I am chosen
(1 Peter 2:9)

I AM WONDERFUL